LAB series

GARDENING LAB
FOR KIDS

Green Gardening

FUN EXPERIMENTS TO LEARN, GROW,
HARVEST, MAKE, AND PLAY

RENATA FOSSEN BROWN

QUARRY

Brimming with creative inspiration, how-to projects, and useful information to enrich your everyday life, Quarto Knows is a favorite destination for those pursuing their interests and passions. Visit our site and dig deeper with our books into your area of interest: Quarto Creates, Quarto Cooks, Quarto Homes, Quarto Lives, Quarto Drives, Quarto Explores, Quarto Gifts, or Quarto Kids.

© 2017 Quarto Publishing Group USA Inc.
Text © 2017 Renata Fossen Brown Photography © 2017 Dave Brown

First Published in 2017 by Quarry Books, an imprint of The Quarto Group, 100 Cummings Center, Suite 265-D, Beverly, MA 01915, USA. T (978) 282-9590 F (978) 283-2742 QuartoKnows.com

Quarry Books titles are also available at discount for retail, wholesale, promotional, and bulk purchase. For details, contact the Special Sales Manager by email at specialsales@quarto.com or by mail at The Quarto Group, Attn: Special Sales Manager, 401 Second Avenue North, Suite 310, Minneapolis, MN 55401, USA.

10 9 8 7 6 5 4 3 2 1

ISBN: 978-1-63159-450-2

Content for this book was originally found in *Gardening Lab for Kids* by Renata Fossen Brown (Quarry Books, 2014)

Cover Image: Dave Brown
Photography: Dave Brown
Illustration: Renata Fossen Brown

Printed in China

* CONTENTS *

* INTRODUCTION *

It's been said that "gardening is better than therapy and you get tomatoes." I would agree. Gardening is also the combination of art and science. This book is a collection of activities I've used both professionally at Cleveland Botanical Garden and personally during the past twenty years. To me, gardening is everything good: exercise (but more fun), being outside (usually), communing with nature, and (hopefully) bettering a tiny patch of earth. I'm not a professional gardener, I'm not a horticulturist, but I do hang out with a bunch of them and ask a lot of questions. The biggest thing I've learned through these interactions is that all of those "rules" they learned in school are simply there to be broken.

Gardening is a personal endeavor, and whatever makes you happy should be what you do. If you love putting pinks and oranges together because they make you smile, then do it. If, instead of the rules of three, you prefer groups of four, then do it.

I get great ideas of things to do in my yard from daily walks with the dogs, plant catalogs, and Pinterest! From these same three places, I also see plenty of things I don't want in my yard. Either way, you learn new things to implement—or not.

* GREEN GARDENING *

You would think that ALL gardening would be considered "green" or good for the planet, right? Most of it certainly is. Anytime you plant a tree, or compost something instead of throwing it out, it is definitely good for the environment. When you learn about and allow wildlife to live in your garden, it helps increase biodiversity, and collecting and using rainwater helps conserve natural resources.

Some people are convinced that to have a beautiful, thriving garden, you must use plenty of man-made fertilizers, potentially dangerous chemicals, and lots of pesticides. This simply isn't true. You can have a gorgeous and successful garden without using any chemicals and absolutely no pesticides. In addition to being much healthier for you and the environment, not using hazardous materials in your yard is also a far cheaper option.

POLLINATOR PALACE

* MATERIALS *

→ Building bricks (the ones with holes)

→ 3 pieces of pegboard, approximately 1' (30 cm) square

→ Many sticks, branches, and twigs, about 1' (30 cm) long

→ 1' (30 cm) pieces of bamboo or other hollow wood

The word *pollinator* refers to any creature that transfers pollen from the flower of one plant to another. Pollinators may be insects, birds, spiders, bats, even people. For this Lab, we are going to focus just on the pollinators with six or more legs. The ideal location for this structure is a spot that gets some sun and some shade, is away from a lot of activity, and is near some plants.

* DIG IN! *

1. In the selected location, lay two bricks down on their sides and lay one piece of pegboard on top of them. Continue with the rest of the bricks and pegboard, ending with a piece of pegboard on top for the roof. (Fig. 1)

Fig. 1: Stack the pegboard and bricks.

Fig. 2: Make sure all the materials fit together tightly.

Fig. 3: Create the roof.

2. Place larger branches in-between the bricks and then add small sticks, twigs, branches, and bamboo into the spaces between the larger branches. Fit everything tightly together so nothing moves around. (Fig. 2)

3. Finish the roof of the palace to prevent too much water from running through: Install more branches on top or get as creative as you want by adding drain tile, roofing shingles, bricks, or more branches. Sit back and wait for your pollinators to take up residence! (Fig. 3)

✳ DIG DEEPER! ✳
HELPFUL POLLINATORS

→ Insects and other pollinators are responsible for pollinating the 100 or so food crops around the world. If it wasn't for them, we wouldn't eat.

→ Domestic honeybee numbers have declined massively in the United States since 2006. Scientists aren't sure why.

→ Providing shelter for bugs can help your garden's health. Obviously, don't use chemicals near your Pollinator Palace—they aren't good for the bugs and they certainly aren't good for you!

* MATERIALS *

→ Plastic "shoebox" type tub, 7" to 8" (18 to 20 cm) tall, with a lid

→ Scratch awl

→ Newspapers

→ Soil

→ Red wigglers

→ Kitchen scraps—vegetable peels, etc.

Worms in your kitchen—yeah!
Although that might sound a bit odd, having a worm bin in your kitchen is a convenient way to keep food scraps out of the landfill while creating "black gold" for your garden: compost! Done correctly, there should be no smell and no fruit flies. The worms you need for this can be obtained from a mail order catalog or a local bait shop. Search on the Internet for "red wigglers" to see where to get them. And then make sure you'll be home when they are delivered!

Fig. 1: Create ventilation holes.

* DIG IN! *

1. Use the scratch awl to poke a line of holes near the top of the container. These are ventilation holes. (Fig. 1)

2. Rip narrow strips of newspaper (don't use the glossy sheets), dip the strips into water, and wring them out. They should be as wet as a damp sponge. This moisture level needs to be maintained, so you may periodically have to spray water into the bin. Ensure there is never standing water at the bottom. (Fig. 2)

3. Fluff up the damp newspaper and place it in the container. This should fill the tub about ¾ full. (Fig. 3)

Fig. 2: Rip and dampen newspaper.

Fig. 3: Add the dampened newspaper to the bin.

Fig. 4: Add soil to the bin.

4. Add two handfuls of moist soil to the tub. This helps the worms digest their food and gives them more places to hide. Add the worms and close the lid. Your worms need some time to adjust to their new "digs" (see what we did there?!), so ignore them for a day or two. Then you can start feeding them. Take pictures daily to document the food scraps disappearing. (Fig. 4)

5. After several weeks, your worms will have created castings (worm poop!) that you can use in your garden. (See opening photo on page 8.)

✳ DIG DEEPER! ✳

CARING FOR YOUR WORMS

→ Things to feed your worms: vegetable and fruit scraps (making sure there is no salad dressing, sauces, or seasonings on them), coffee grounds, wet bread, or cooked pasta.

→ Things not to feed your worms: meat, sugar, salt, citrus, dairy, and processed foods. The smaller the scraps are that you put into the bin, the faster they will begin to decompose, and the sooner your worms will start to eat them.

→ Once you become a pro worm-keeper, your worms will reproduce, increasing your population. Because these worms are adapted to living in a very rich, fluffy, organic place, they may not do well if released into your outdoor garden. The best thing to do with an overabundance of worms is to either start an additional worm bin or give some to a friend so that he or she can start a worm bin. What a great gift, right?

* MATERIALS *

→ 10" (25 cm) clay pot

→ Paints

→ Paint brushes

→ Clear polyurethane sealer

→ Trowel

Toads (and their close relatives, frogs) are very important for the ecosystem. Both animals' main diet consists of insects, many of which are pests to food crops, such as aphids or slugs. Wouldn't it be great to attract them to your yard to keep an eye on your garden?

Fig. 1: Decorate the pot, let dry, add sealer, and let dry.

Fig. 2: Dig a small area for the pot.

1. Paint some fun designs on the clay pot and let it dry. Apply the sealer and let dry overnight. (Fig. 1)

2. Find a shady, out-of-the-way location in your garden for your toad abode. Using the trowel, dig a slight depression in the soil so that when you lay the pot on its side, it won't roll around. (Fig. 2)

3. Lay the pot on its side in the depression you dug. Fill the area around the pot with soil so that the pot will stay in place. (See photo on page 10.)

* DIG DEEPER! *

HEALTHY TOADS, HEALTHY ENVIRONMENT

→ Both frogs and toads are amphibians, and are key indicators of a healthy environment. Why? Because they breathe and absorb water through their skin! If the environment is polluted, they ingest those pollutants, which can kill them or prevent them from reproducing.

→ If you aren't seeing frogs or toads in your neighborhood when there should be some around, there could be something wrong. Lawn chemicals, pollution, or acid rain could be some of the reasons.

* MATERIALS *

→ 55 gallon (208 L) barrel (make sure it is "food-grade" and cleaned thoroughly)

→ ¹⁵/₁₆" (24 mm) drill bit and drill

→ ¾" (2 cm) pipe tap (These are about $25 and can be found at hardware stores. See if you can borrow one from someone instead of buying one.)

→ ¾" (2 cm) male spigot (boiler drain)

→ ¾" (2 cm) thread (male) to ½" (1.3 cm) hose connection hose barb

→ Teflon tape

→ Crescent wrench

→ Diverter kit (see Resources on page 31)

Rain barrels are a great way to harvest FREE water for use in your garden. The average gardener can save more than 1,000 gallons (3785 L) of water each summer by installing and using a rain barrel—it saves natural resources and lots of money, too. Imagine all of the new plants you could buy with those savings!

* DIG IN! *

1. With a ¹⁵/₁₆" (24 mm) drill bit, drill one hole near the bottom of the barrel for the spigot (boiler drain). Drill a second hole near the top of the barrel for the hose barb. Keep in mind which side you want the top hole on to connect to the diverter from the downspout. The top hole that you drill may be on the opposite side of the barrel as the bottom hole. (Fig. 1)

2. Thread both holes with the ¾" (2 cm) pipe tap. This creates ridges in the holes for the spigot and hose barb to be tightly inserted into the rain barrel and seal against water leaking. (Fig. 2)

3. Wrap the threaded ends of the spigot and hose barb with Teflon tape. (Fig. 3)

4. Insert the spigot and hose barb into their correct holes. Use the wrench to tighten and secure them into place. (Fig. 4)

5. Cut the downspout and attach the diverter according to the kit directions, fitting the hose into the hose barb. Water will continue flowing through the downspout, but now some will also be diverted into the barrel. Paint your rain barrel. (Fig. 5)

Fig. 1: Drill holes for the spigot and hose barb.

Fig. 2: Thread both holes with the pipe tap.

Fig. 3: Tape the ends of the spigot and hose barb.

Fig. 4: Tighten and secure the spigot and hose barb.

TIP: You'll need to elevate your rain barrel (cinder blocks work well for this) for several reasons:

• The higher the rain barrel is, the better water pressure you will get.

• Putting your rain barrel on stable ground and elevated will prevent it from sinking into the ground. A filled barrel weighs more than 400 lbs (181 kg).

• If the rain barrel is too close to the ground, you won't be able to fit a watering can under the spout.

Fig. 5: Attach the diverter to the cut downspout and insert.

⁕ DIG DEEPER! ⁕

MAINTAIN YOUR RAIN BARREL

→ If you live in a climate with winters below freezing, you'll need to disconnect your rain barrel each fall and store it for the season. This is a good time to empty it and clean it all out so it will be ready for the spring.

→ To further save water, use mulch in your garden to slow water evaporation from the soil and keep your plants nice and happy.

→ Get artistic with your rain barrel and paint a design on it! (See photo on page 12 for inspiration!)

* MATERIALS *

→ 3 wooden pallets

→ Paint (lots of different colors, exterior house paint works best)

→ Paint brush that will get trashed

→ 4 corner braces, screws, and screwdriver and/or drill

→ Gloves (optional)

Decide on the location for your compost bin. It should receive some sunlight and not be right next to the house. Also consider that how you paint your compost bin may depend on how often you see it. You may not want crazy colors staring back at you when you look outside!

TIP: Ask your local grocer or store manager for wooden pallets; most of the time they are glad to see them go to a good home. Pallets can be very rough and cause splinters, so you may want to wear gloves when handling them.

Fig. 1: Paint one side of each pallet.

* DIG IN! *

1. Paint one side of each of the pallets and let dry. You can paint it all one color or get creative. Only paint the outside of the compost bin. (Fig. 1)

2. Your pallets will be the sides of your bin (it will be open at the bottom). Assemble them at right angles and insert the screws and braces into the corners. (Fig. 2)

Fig. 2: Assemble the sides and attach them with braces.

Fig. 3: Add green plant material.

Fig. 4: Turn your compost regularly.

3. Start filling the bin. First add about 6" (15 cm) of small sticks and branches at the bottom to help with drainage.

4. On top of this, add 6" (15 cm) of fresh plant material, such as dried leaves or sticks. Then add 3" (8 cm) of fresh plant material, such as green leaves, grass clippings, weeds (without seeds), or kitchen scraps. (Fig. 3)

5. Use a pitchfork or shovel to mix the pile once a week for speedier results and to prevent stinky conditions. After several weeks, you'll be able to collect fantastic, homemade compost from the bottom of the pile to use in your garden. (Fig. 4)

✴ DIG DEEPER! ✴

TAKING THE STINK OUT OF COMPOSTING

Some people don't compost because they think it is "stinky." Actually, if you compost correctly, there is no smell. There should be a combination of two parts brown things (e.g., dried leaves) to one part green things (e.g., kitchen compost). Your compost pile should also stay moist and will heat up from all of the microbes busy eating away in the pile. Too many grass clippings decreases the amount of air spaces in the pile and can create anaerobic conditions, causing a stinky pile.

* MATERIALS *

→ Pieces of redwood or cedar: For this window, we obtained one piece of cedar 1" x 12" x 8' (2.5 x 30 x 244 cm) for the back and two sides, and one piece of cedar 1" x 8" x 2' (2.5 x 20 x 61 cm) for the front.

→ Straight edge

→ Pencil

→ Circular saw

→ 8 corner wood braces

→ 32 wood screws

→ Screwdriver

→ 2 hinges and screws

→ 1 old glass window (this one measured 21" x 27" (53 x 68.5 cm)

→ 10" to 12" (25 to 30 cm) stick

A cold frame is an enclosure used to protect plants from cold weather. It has a transparent top to allow sunlight in to warm the plants inside, acting like a small greenhouse. Cold frames aren't used during warm summer months (it would be too hot for plant growth), just during cooler times of year. They help gardeners get a jump on the upcoming growing season and to grow things later into the fall. Select a location for your cold frame—a south-facing side of a building is best.

Fig. 5: Prop open the cold frame on warm days.

Note: When using an old window, make sure it doesn't contain lead paint or pressure-treated wood. When purchasing wood, measure around all sides of the window; that is the total length of wood you will need. For example, if the window is 3' (91 cm) long and 2' (61 cm) wide, you would need 10' (305 cm) of wood (3 + 3 + 2 + 2 = 10).

* DIG IN! *

Fig. 1: Measure each side piece and draw a cutting guide.

1. Start making the box frame. Because the window will be tilted down in front slightly, the two side pieces of wood will be cut at an angle. The front of the side pieces will be the height of the front board; the back of the side pieces will angle up to the height of the back board. Measure and mark each side piece accordingly. Use a straight edge to draw a straight line from this mark to the top of the other end, creating an angled piece of wood. (Fig. 1)

2. With adult assistance, use a circular saw to cut each of the four pieces of wood along the line you drew. (Fig. 2)

Fig. 2: Cut the four pieces of wood.

Fig. 3: Attach the wood pieces.

Fig. 4: Attach the hinges to the frame and the window.

3. Position each piece of wood at a right angle to the next to create an angled box with the tallest piece of wood as the back of the cold frame. Fasten a corner wood brace 1" (2.5 cm) from the top and 1" (2.5 cm) from the bottom inside each corner. Use the wood screws and a screw driver to attach the pieces to each other. (Fig. 3)

4. Attach the hinges to the outside, top back of the frame, then attach the window to the hinges. (Fig. 4) Place plants inside the cold frame. On warmer or sunnier days, use a stick to prop the window up a bit so it doesn't get too hot inside and bake your plants. (See photo on page 16.)

* DIG DEEPER! *
EXTEND THE SEASON

→ Making a cold frame can be as simple or as complicated as you wish to make it. We are doing a very simple version of one here, and once you get the idea, you can experiment with building something different.

→ Unless you live in an area where you can grow year-round, you might want to investigate how to grow things earlier in the season as well as later in the season. This is called "season extension," and your cold frame can help you do it.

→ Because of the window acting as a lid, rain won't be able to enter the cold frame. This means you are responsible for watering any plants inside. During very cool months, many plants are dormant and don't need much, if any, water.

* MATERIALS *

→ Wire hanger

→ Duct tape

→ ¾" (2 cm) wooden dowel

→ 1 yard (91.5 cm) tulle fabric

→ Needle and thread

→ Small, clean glass jar with lid (poke small holes in the lid)

→ Insect identification book or insect ID app on a mobile device

Bugs are incredibly important to a successful garden, and most bugs you find in a garden are beneficial, or good, bugs. Take some time to introduce yourself to your insect residents and learn a little bit about them.

Fig. 1: Tightly tape the straight part of the hanger to the dowel rod.

* DIG IN! *

1. "Round out" the triangle part of the wire clothes hanger, straighten out the hook part, and duct tape like crazy the now straight part to the wooden dowel. (Fig. 1)

2. Fold the tulle in half and cut a triangle as shown. Stitch the long open sides together. (Fig. 2)

3. Fold the circular opening of the net over the round part of the wire hanger, overlapping by 1" (2.5 cm). Stitch all the way around to hold it in place. You now have an insect net! (Fig. 3)

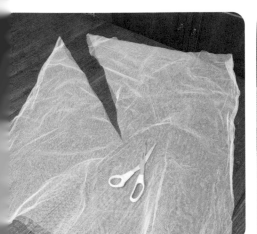

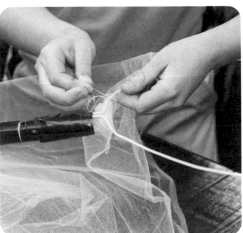

Fig. 2: Fold and cut fabric to form a "cone."

Fig. 3: Loop fabric over the wire hanger and sew it in place.

Fig. 4: Identify the bug in the jar and release it when done.

4. In the garden, use a gentle sweeping motion of the net to capture an insect you want to closely study, as shown in the opening photo on page 18. Gently deposit the insect you catch into the glass jar and close the lid. Use your ID guides to find out what kind of insect you captured. It is probably a "good guy," so open the lid and put him back where you captured him and say thank you! (Fig. 4)

✳ DIG DEEPER! ✳
CREATE A BUG-FRIENDLY GARDEN

Encourage helpful insects to visit your garden by growing plants they need to live. For example, to attract lacewings to your yard, plant fennel, yarrow, or dill. Lady beetles (lady bugs) also love a good yarrow or dill, in addition to Queen Anne's lace and coriander. An additional bonus is that these plants that attract beneficial insects are lovely as well!

* MATERIALS *

→ Old wooden picture frame about 8" x 10" (20 x 25.4 cm)

→ Drill and tiny drill bit

→ 4 small screw eyes

→ Piece of screening slightly bigger than your picture frame

→ Staple gun and staples

→ 5 small "S" hooks

→ 10' (304 cm) of rope chain

Bird watching is the number one activity in many parts of the world, and it's easy to see why. Birds come in all colors and sizes, and their behaviors are interesting and sometimes comical to watch! By making a feeder for the birds and hanging it near a window, you can attract them close for convenient, indoor viewing.

* DIG IN! *

1. Drill guide holes in each corner on the back of the picture frame. (Fig. 1)

2. Using the holes you drilled, set the screw eyes into place. (Fig. 2)

3. Center the screening over the picture frame. Use the staple gun to fix it in place. Make sure you staple the screening near the corners of the frame. (Fig. 3)

Fig. 1: Drill the guide holes.

Fig. 2: Insert the screw eyes.

Fig. 3: Center and staple the screening into the frame.

Fig. 4: Attach the rope chain to the feeder.

4. Loop an "S" hook through each screw eye. Then loop a 2' (61 cm) section of rope chain through each "S" hook, gathering each piece together and looping them through the fifth "S" hook. Hang the feeder by attaching the rest of the rope to the "S" hook. Fill the feeder with seed and hang outside to enjoy. Your feathered friends will thank you. (Fig. 4)

* DIG DEEPER! *
HELP NATIVE BIRDS

→ Research the native birds of your area; a good place to start is your state's department of natural resources website. Learn what your native birds need for survival and help provide that for them. Planting perennials, shrubs, and trees that provide food and shelter for them year-round is ideal. Provide clean water for them to drink and bathe in by making your own birdbath.

→ Native birds are important to the ecosystem as pollinators, insect and rodent control, distributing seeds, and many other reasons. The biggest threat to native birds is the domestic cat. Cats kill millions of songbirds every year. The best way to prevent this is to keep cats indoors, which keeps cats safe, too.

Most of us are not blessed with weather that allows us to garden outside year-round. But you can still get your plant fix by gardening indoors. Use a container that has a wide opening so you don't have to cut the top to get all of your materials inside. Make sure you've cleaned the container well with soap and water before starting.

* MATERIALS *

→ Sheet of paper

→ Clear, lidded plastic or glass bottle with large top opening

→ 2 cups (490 g) gravel

→ 1 to 3 tablespoons (30 to 90 g) charcoal

→ 2 cups (200 g) potting soil

→ Chopstick or other long stick

→ Cuttings from plants to propagate: Jade (Crassula), Snake plant (Sansevieria), Burro's tail (Sedum)

→ Rooting powder

→ Spray bottle

* DIG IN! *

1. Roll the paper into a funnel shape and use it to pour the gravel into the bottom of your terrarium. Gently shake bottle to spread the gravel evenly. (Fig. 1)

Fig. 1 (left): Pour in the gravel.

Fig. 2: Pour in the charcoal and soil.

Fig. 3: Dip the cuttings.

Fig. 4: Lower each plant into the bottle.

2. Pour charcoal onto the gravel, using a chopstick to spread it evenly on top. Pour the soil in the same way. (Fig. 2)

3. Decide how you want your plants arranged. Dip the stem of each plant cutting into the rooting powder. Follow directions and precautions listed on the rooting powder container. (Fig. 3)

4. Lower each plant into its location. (Fig. 4)

5. Press plants firmly into the soil, using your chopsticks. Spray water all over the inside of the bottle and put the lid back on your terrarium. (Fig. 5)

Fig. 5: Use the chopsticks to move the plants into location.

||||||||||||||||||||||||||| * DIG DEEPER! * |||||||||||||||||||||||||||

HOW TO WATER YOUR TERRARIUM

→ One of the coolest things about terraria (plural of terrarium) is that if done correctly, they require almost no care. It's important to put the right amounts of gravel and soil in the container you choose. The soil will hold moisture in it and the gravel helps drain too much water away to prevent your plants from getting waterlogged.

→ Newly propagated plants (like the cuttings we used here) need a bit more water when they are first planted, so growing them in a terrarium is perfect. The day after you plant them, check the terrarium to see how much water is on the sides of the container. If all of the sides are covered in big water drops, there is too much water in your terrarium. This is easily fixed by taking the lid off the container for several hours, then replacing it.

* MATERIALS *

→ Dryer lint

→ Small sticks

→ Dried grass

→ Short pieces of yarn

→ Large metal whisk

→ 8" (20 cm) piece of twine

Home is where the heart is, but when it comes to birds, home is where the nest is. Many birds use various materials to make their nests where they lay eggs and protect their young. Birds are busy, so why not collect those items for them and keep them all together in one place?

* DIG IN! *

1. Gather the miscellaneous nesting materials by searching around the yard or in the neighborhood. When collecting dried grass, do not take it from lawns that have chemicals on them. Break or cut small sticks so they are shorter than 6" (15 cm) long. Cotton yarn should be cut into pieces smaller than 4" (10 cm). (Fig. 1)

2. Push all of the materials into the whisk. Tie the twine through the handle and hang the whisk from a tree birds like to visit (maybe near the bird feeder you made in Lab 8?). (Fig. 2)

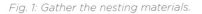

Fig. 1: Gather the nesting materials.

Fig. 2: Insert the nesting materials.

✳ DIG DEEPER! ✳
FOR THE BIRDS

→ It is believed that birds evolved from dinosaurs. Makes you want to give them a little more respect, doesn't it?

→ Birds have hollow bones so they are lightweight and can fly.

→ Attracting birds to your garden is a win-win: Birds are so entertaining to watch, and insect-eating birds will help remove pests from your plants.

BONUS LABS

FLOWER ARRANGEMENT

* MATERIALS *

→ Empty spaghetti sauce jar, label removed

→ Pruners

→ Bunch of small sticks that are fairly straight

→ Waterproof silicone adhesive

→ Twine

→ Sharp scissors

→ Flowers from your garden or permission to harvest someone else's

Who doesn't like to get flowers? And giving them is just as fun—especially when the flowers are gifts from your very own garden. Before starting, wash the sauce jar well and remove the label. You may need to soak it in hot, soapy water to remove the label glue.

‖‖‖ * DIG IN! * ‖‖‖

1. Using the pruners, cut the sticks to the height of the glass jar. Apply a bead of silicone to the outside of the jar and press a stick into it. Continue around the entire jar, creating a fence look, and let it dry for a few hours or overnight. (Fig. 1)

2. Cut two 20" (51 cm) pieces of twine to wrap around and tie at the top and bottom of the jar. This will help hold the sticks in place. (Fig. 2)

3. When you are ready to harvest your flowers, carefully fill your jar halfway with clean, lukewarm water. Avoid getting the glued sticks wet. Collect your flowers first thing in the morning if possible so that they last longer. Cut the stems at a 45° angle. This opens up the most surface area for the stem to take up water. (Fig. 3) Arrange the tallest flowers in the middle of the jar, with shorter flowers around them. Use some leaves around the outer edge for a nice border, and voila! You have a beautiful, handmade creation for someone special (or yourself)!

Fig. 1: Glue the twigs around the jar.

Fig. 2: Tie twine around the jar.

Fig. 3: Cut flower stems at an angle.

* DIG DEEPER! *
WHAT DO YOUR FLOWERS SAY TO YOU?

Did you know that flowers have different meanings? Long ago in Victorian times, people would sometimes communicate their feelings through the flowers they sent someone. It was like a code to figure out what a bouquet of different flowers meant! Depending on the source you use, flowers can mean all sorts of different things. Here is just a sampling—read *The Language of Flowers* for more!

Daisy: Innocence
Red rose: Love
Yellow rose: Friendship
Rosemary: Remembrance
Violet: Modesty, loyalty, devotion
Zinnia: Thoughts of friends

* DIG EVEN DEEPER! *
PRESERVING FLOWERS

Experiment to see what can be added to the water to preserve cut flowers the longest. Line up a bunch of clean jars and add the same amount of water and same kinds of flower to each. Add lemon juice to one, sugar to one, bleach to one, and so on, and see which keeps your flowers fresh the longest. Start a garden journal and make note of this, to tell all your friends!

MAKE A PLANT PRESS

* MATERIALS *

→ Plant specimens

→ 2 wood pieces, 1' (30 cm) square

→ 6 to 10 pieces of corrugated cardboard, slightly smaller than 1' (30 cm) square

→ Newspaper

→ 2 webbing belts (also called utility straps)

Many people are attracted to certain plants because of their flowers. People go crazy over orchid flowers or roses. I'm a sucker for leaves. Coleus, hosta, maple, and spider plant leaves will stop me in my tracks. So many different shapes and sizes and colors, oh my! I can't get enough of them. This is where pressing leaves comes in handy. You can gather leaves any time of year, press them, and use them to display or as a part of gifts. And of course, you can press flowers too!

Fig. 1: Collect your plant specimens.

* DIG IN! *

1. Collect your plant parts for pressing. Leaves and flowers that are very thick might not press well, but why not experiment anyway? (Fig. 1)

2. Once you are ready to press your specimens, lay one piece of cardboard on top of one piece of wood, followed by two sheets of newspaper. (Fig. 2)

3. Carefully place one leaf or flower on top of the newspaper, then lay two more sheets of paper on top. Repeat the cardboard and newspaper layers (one piece of cardboard, two sheets of newspaper, one plant specimen, two more sheets of newspaper) until you use your last piece of cardboard. Place the second piece of wood on top. (Fig. 3)

Fig. 2: Start building your press.

Fig. 3: Sandwich your plant samples between newspaper and cardboard.

Fig. 4: Tighten the webbing belts.

4. Wrap the webbing belts around the whole thing and pull the belts tight. Place your plant press in a dry place. It will take several days to absorb the moisture out of the specimens and flatten them out. After about a week, undo the belts and gently lift the newspapers away from your leaves. They are ready to display or use in crafts. (Fig. 4)

＊ DIG DEEPER! ＊
CREATE AN HERBARIUM SHEET

You can use your preserved specimens for crafts or to display or for any number of things. You could also create herbarium sheets: Mount the specimen on paper and write all of the information about the plant, including date and time of collection. Natural history museums and other research institutions make and keep herbarium sheets as a way to document changes in plant populations. For example, they can go back 100 years and look up an herbarium sheet on a plant to see its original range, or region it could be found in, and compare that with the current day. This gives researchers information on climate change, plant diseases, and so on.

* RESOURCES *

Gardening Information

Heat zones in the United States:
American Horticultural Society
www.ahs.org

Outside the United States, find your hardiness zone here:
www.backyardgardener.com/zone/#outside

Order trees and get tons of useful information:
Arbor Day Foundation
www.arborday.org

List of plants that can be toxic to dogs and cats:
The American Society for the Prevention of Cruelty to Animals
www.aspca.org

Tips on planting, insects, and gardening:
Ohio State Extension
www.ohioline.osu.edu

Tools and Supplies

Garden trowel:
Radius Garden
www.radiusgarden.com

Diverter kit for rain barrels:
Garden Water Saver
http://gardenwatersaver.com

My favorite place to order seeds:
Johnny's Selected Seeds
www.johnnyseeds.com

My favorite place to order perennials:
Bluestone Perennials
www.bluestoneperennials.com

Miniatures and craft items:
Pat Catan's Craft Centers
www.patcatans.com

* ABOUT THE AUTHOR *

As the Vice President of Education, Renata Fossen Brown oversees the thousands of school children visiting Cleveland Botanical Garden yearly, the development and implementation of teacher professional development workshops, the library, Hershey Children's Garden, and the garden's urban youth farming program, Green Corps. She assisted in the planning and facilitating of a ten-day teacher workshop in Costa Rica to study biodiversity. Brown is involved in the writing of interpretation and exhibit graphics at the garden and served as president of the Cleveland Regional Council of Science Teachers.

Brown holds a B.A. in biology from the University of Toledo and an M.A. in curriculum and instruction from Bradley University, in Peoria, Ill. She is certified to teach grades seven through twelve science, and has been active in informal science education since 1993.

As Assistant Curator of Education at the Toledo Zoo, Brown was responsible for all educational programs occurring on zoo grounds, as well as researching and writing for the zoo's Emmy award-winning television show, *Zoo Today*. Creating and implementing its very first Earth Day celebration is a task of which she is particularly proud. She continued her education role, while adding volunteer coordinator duties and working at Luthy Botanical Garden in Peoria.

A native Clevelander, Renata Fossen Brown gladly returned home in 2004 after a fifteen-year absence. She was named the garden's Clara DeMallie Sherwin Chair in Education in December 2004. She is usually surrounded in her yard by her three dogs and prefers natives and perennials over annuals any day. She is particularly in love with purple coneflower.

www.cbgarden.org

* ACKNOWLEDGMENTS *

Most importantly, thank you to all of my friends and neighbors who let me borrow their children for the creation of this book. Every single one of them amazed me and cracked me up.

To the staff of Cleveland Botanical Garden for giving advice, answering questions, and allowing me the opportunity to write this book, I thank you. Natalie, Ann, Larry, Kathryn, and Geri: Thank you for your support and wisdom.

Many thanks to the Cuyahoga County Soil and Water Conservation District for the hundreds of rain barrels they get out into the community each year and their help with Lab 4!

To the ladies of the Western Reserve Herb Society—you're fantastic and you gave me great ideas, along with a chuckle or two.

To Mary Ann Hall at Quarry Books—thank you for looking me up and giving me such a great opportunity. Your personality made this whole process quite wonderful.

Finally to my husband Dave, who named tools and equipment and gadgets for me, bounced ideas around, walked the dogs when I needed to work, and took absolutely fantastic pictures. Thank you for your patience and support.